TIMELESS PLACES

MOROCCO

ANNETTE SOLYST

BARNES
&NOBLE
BOOKS
NEW YORK

A BARNES & NOBLE BOOK

©2000 by Michael Friedman Publishing Group, Inc.

ISBN 0-7607-4519-6

Editors: Ann Kirby-Payne and Alexandra Bonfante-Warren
Art Director: Jeff Batzli
Designer: John Marius
Photography Editor: Kate Perry
Production Managers: Richela Fabian-Morgan, Camille Lee, and Maria Gonzalez

Color separations by Spectrum Pte. Ltd.
Printed in Hong Kong by Midas Printing Limited

3 5 7 9 10 8 6 4 2

PAGE 1: **The Portuguese fortified Essaouira, the old Mogador, its solid walls built in the 1760s. Through the gates, lanes lead to sunny open squares and thuya wood workshops, where furniture is handmade, and the clinking of hammers and the pungent fragrance of fresh wood leave a lasting impression.**
PAGES 2–3: **East of Ouarzazate lies the Skoura oasis. Intensively cultivated, with every bit of arable land used by the palmery, the road leads to a group of casbahs. Portions of the buildings date back to the 1600s, although most of them were built over the past one hundred years. They do not stand the test of time gracefully, as inclement weather is highly destructive to the mud walls.**

CONTENTS

PAGE 4: **The mules and donkeys of the
High Atlas Berbers are beasts of burden as well as
transportation. Taking sacks of barley to market,
man and mule patiently tread the passageways
through the mountains, regions that have few
paved roads or vehicles, and no need for them.**

PAGE 5: **Intricate, time-honored geometric motifs
and a wrought-iron fixture grace a door. Just as
prayers punctuate the hours, so ceremony adorns
everyday objects.**

RIGHT: **Morocco without spices is like an ocean
without fish—simply unimaginable. Senses come
alive with the fragrances of saffron and turmeric
mingling with cumin and cinnamon. The entire
country seems to be scented by spices!**

PART 1
STORY

"Like any romantic," wrote the novelist Paul Bowles, "I had been certain that sometime in my life I should come into a magic place which in disclosing its secrets would give me wisdom and ecstasy." Morocco moved Bowles to write these words, and his sentiments echo those of many travelers who have ventured into this seductive, mysterious realm.

Morocco's magic can overwhelm even the most practical sensibility. European shores, though so close (Spain is just nine miles [13km] across the Strait of Gibraltar), seem far removed as the sights, smells, and textures of North Africa welcome the traveler. To the Western eye, the people themselves seem exotic. Traditionally garbed men wear long, hooded robes, or djellabas, while women may be draped in blue haiks, their faces veiled with black scarves that leave only their dark, kohl-rimmed eyes visible. The mountain, desert, and ocean vistas reveal nature's inexorable forces at work, while in the towns, bustling markets give way to narrow alleys down which a traveler might find small, cavelike, and possibly magical shops selling rare powders and spices, or even a jinn embodying the ancient power of Morocco.

❧

PAGES 8–9: In the distance, the snow-capped Atlas Mountains loom, cool and impressive. On the Haouz Plain, miles of twelfth-century walls with ten massive gates enclose the old part of Marrakech. Nearby, a domed entry gate and wall are decorated with geometric brickwork.

OPPOSITE: Like a sandcastle, this Dades Valley casbah rises before rolling hills, giving shelter to the large Berber clan that makes its home there. Built like a fortress along rectangular lines, its walls slant slightly outward. Corner towers are characteristic of casbahs, as is a single large gateway that could be shut in case of attack.

Forming the northwestern corner of the African continent, the Kingdom of Morocco is renowned for its dramatic and diverse countryside. Three imposing chains of the Atlas Mountains cross the country from the northeast to the southwest. Their most prominent mountain peak, Mount Toubkal, is the highest point in all of North Africa and is known by the Berber people as *Adrar n' Deren*, or "Mountain of Mountains." Along the northern coastline, another mountain range, the Rif, forms a magnificent backdrop to the sandy beaches of the Mediterranean. The Atlantic Ocean laps Morocco's western shores, while the forbidding Sahara Desert, sprinkled with oases rich in date palms, lies to the south. Figs, tangerines, and pomegranates grow wild while oranges, olives, cork trees, and bananas are cultivated on fertile land. From the royal cities of Fez, Meknès, Rabat, and Marrakech to the hamlets dotting the countryside, colorful *souks*—traditional Moroccan markets—invite browsing among the goods grown and crafted in the country.

The Rif and the massive Atlas ranges divide Morocco into distinct sections, isolating valleys and people. Barley and maize grow tenuously on carefully tended terraces on mountain slopes and along riverbeds, painting farmed plots a lush springtime green. Endless rolling fields of grain wave in the wind in the northern regions. Landscapes such as these have distinctly shaped the people who call this country their home.

Earth, wind, fire, and water—all elements are represented here, often in extremes. Arid southern *chergui* winds blow the Sahara's burning heat inland. During the hot season, the sun shines mercilessly, drying out riverbeds and scorching the earth until deep cracks appear in the soil. The land is tanned in hues of beige, brown, copper, and rose, overlaid with a fine layer of powdery dust. The scent of sun-baked earth fills the air. Without warning, a sudden sandstorm can blind travelers, halting them in their tracks. From the west, cold *gharbi* winter winds drench the Atlas Mountains, bringing moisture to the plateaus and valleys, nourishing cedars and grazing land, filling creek beds and rivulets, and, in the higher elevations, turning rain into snow. During the cold season, mountain passes may be blocked by snow that later melts, revitalizing the plains below.

The wind creates gentle ripples and waves of sand, endlessly changing and reshaping the contours of the desert, like a living work of abstract art. Serenity and timelessness emanate from the vast dunes, casting a spell on visitor and desert dweller alike.

Cities by the Sea

The seas that border Morocco along the north and west coasts have always been its connection to the world. This region was once known as the Barbary Coast, land of adventurers and pirates. As long ago as 1000 B.C.E. the sea brought the Phoenicians, who established the ports of Tingis (Tangier) and Mogador (Essaouira). Throughout the Mediterranean these famous seafarers traded in goods such as cedar wood, glass, spices, and perfumes. Tangier's strategic location on the Strait of Gibraltar made it a much-coveted town. The Romans, Visigoths, Arabs, Spanish, and French ruled in succession, each leaving their mark on the city. From 1923 until Morocco's independence from the French in 1956, Tangier was an international zone, governed by diplomatic agents from several European nations and the United States. Dubbed "Interzone" by the writer William S. Burroughs, Tangier earned a shady reputation as a place where illegal activities and clandestine acts were part of everyday life. Much lore surrounds this era of profiteering, money laundering, smuggling, and intrigue. Even today, the city is home to some of Morocco's most enthusiastic and adept hustlers and pickpockets. Yet in spite of this dubious distinction (or perhaps because of it), Tangier has an enduring charm all its own.

Tangier's hilly medina, the old Arab city, invites exploration. Small enough for wanderers to simply meander down its streets, it is a visual delight. Wrought-iron window guards

and wooden shutters reveal the influence of Spanish rule during the sixteenth and seventeenth centuries. Vines and bushes eke out a hard-fought existence amid cracking ramparts. The city's ancient walls act as a foundation for its houses. Squeezed close together and flat-roofed in typical North African style, the homes resemble a Cubist painting come to life. Steep steps lead up to whimsical portals, where blue and yellow tiles in medallion motifs frame Moorish arches.

No doubt Tangier's importance as a commercial center is due to its strategic proximity to the Atlantic as well as to the Strait of Gibraltar. The port has played a major role in this. It came into prominence in the fourteenth century, as Tangier developed into a trading hub for the Mediterranean world. The seafaring nations of Spain, Portugal, and Great Britain had a presence here and utilized the port.

Follow the labyrinthine streets, past shops selling colorful carpets, to reach the *Petit Socco*, the medina's small central square. Bustling with people, the square is the perfect place to take in the flavor of a Tangier day from one of the many cafés. Sitting outdoors, sipping strong black coffee, local patrons at nearby tables sport ankle-length djellabas, pointed leather slippers, and intricately crocheted skullcaps. Further into the medina, continuing up steep cobbled lanes, the historic casbah sits on sheer cliffs high over the Strait of Gibraltar. From this beautiful lookout point, musicians can be heard playing hauntingly stirring music for the visitors who have come to sit and while away the hours.

haunches by the sidewalk, selling produce. The fragrance of freshly cut mint mingles with the aroma of cone-shaped mounds of spices—yellow turmeric, brown cinnamon, and bright red paprika—and invites the cook to linger.

For centuries, artists have found inspiration in Morocco, praising the clarity of the light and the distinctive images that they encountered there. Early in his career, painter Henri Matisse delighted in the vivid yet subtle colors and bold architecture he saw during his visits to Tangier. Word spread among writers as well, drawn by long-time resident Paul Bowles; other notable literary visitors include Tennessee Williams and Gore Vidal. The Beat poets were especially

Not surprisingly, ancient Tangier, with its confluence of cultures and exotic setting, is a feast for the senses. Nowhere is this more evident than in Tangier's many markets, where mounds of olives in shades of green and black are piled high, and women with wide-brimmed straw hats sit on their

attracted to Tangier—William S. Burroughs arrived in the late 1950s to write *Naked Lunch*, followed by Allen Ginsberg, Jack Kerouac, and Brion Gysin. The wealthy jet set came to town in the 1950s and '60s, led by Woolworth heiress Barbara Hutton, whose villa in the medina was the scene of

Ceuta, on the northern tip of Morocco, has been a Spanish enclave since 1580. From these sandy beaches, boats ply the waters of the Strait of Gibraltar: the Rock is visible from here. Though on African soil, Ceuta's clocks tick on Spanish time—a two-hour difference.

elaborate parties that lasted for days. That era may be long gone, but Hutton's house can still be seen from a nearby café overlooking the premises.

Hardly an hour south of Tangier is Asilah, a small seaside town with a remarkably eventful past. Founded by the Carthaginians some two thousand years ago, it subsequently fell to the Romans. During the Punic Wars, the residents of Asilah supported the losing side. In an effort to punish the population, the Romans shipped them into slavery in Spain and brought Iberians to take their place. In the tenth century, Asilah fought off Norman invaders. Finally, in 1471, the Portuguese took over. They built the fortified walls that still surround the town, but a mere hundred years later they lost Asilah to the Spanish. After changing hands several more times, Asilah was finally turned over to Morocco in 1691. In recent years, the town has become an elegant resort, a holiday spot for myriad wealthy Moroccans and Europeans. It is also home to a number of artists from all over the world.

Perhaps the most colorful part of Asilah's history centers on turn-of-the-twentieth-century brigand Raissouli. For a short while he ruled as *pasha* of the town, but his penchant for banditry never weakened. He graduated from petty theft to murder to what would become his most profitable and well-known form of lawlessness: his habit of kidnapping Westerners. In the early 1900s, he and his band snatched and held for ransom various foreign luminaries, including London *Times* correspondent Walter Harris and naturalized American Ion Perdicaris, sparking international crises. Such antics interfered with his political ambitions, eventually landing him in

disfavor with the country's leaders, and also in jail. Raissouli's palace in Asilah has been beautifully preserved and is one of the city's more picturesque sights.

South along the Atlantic, Rabat and Casablanca form the two major centers of activity in the central coastal area. The nation's capital, Rabat, seat of the government and home to the king, is many visitors' first glimpse of Morocco. Primarily a modern city, its wide boulevards and many gardens inspired by Andalusia give it an unhurried yet cosmopolitan air. The most famous landmark is the Tour Hassan, a minaret dating to the twelfth century. Rabat's medina, originally settled by Muslims and Jews driven out of Spain, is a surprising contrast to the international flair of the Ville Nouvelle, or "New City." Along its eastern edge is the mellah, the old Jewish quarter. Here, as in other Moroccan cities, the Jewish population declined significantly after 1948 when many Jews emigrated to Israel.

Located within minutes of the city's ramparts are the remains of the ancient Roman city of Sala Colonia, which became the Berber city of Chella and, under the Merinides, the necropolis of Chella. Considered to be the most beautiful of all Moroccan ruins, it was a thriving city for a thousand years until 1154 C.E., when it was abandoned in favor of neighboring Sale. Ruins of a Roman villa, baths, a forum, and a temple can be viewed inside its walls. Beginning in the 1200s, Chella was used as a cemetery by the ruling dynasties of the country.

In contrast to Rabat, Casablanca astounds with its fast pace and its affinity for Western ways. Perhaps the best known of any Moroccan city—thanks to Michael Curtiz's 1942 film of the same name—Casablanca is also the most contemporary. Classic Art Deco architecture attests to the area's growth in the early days of the French protectorate. Even more striking is the lifestyle of the city's residents: modern dress is common and veils are rare. Women and men socialize together as easily as in Europe's most cosmopolitan cities. A hub of Moroccan commerce and industry, Casablanca is home to nearly four million people.

Moving south from the coastline of central Morocco, another ancient settlement beckons in Essaouira. What the Phoenicians recognized as an ideal trading post and the Romans celebrated as a source of precious purple dye is now a windsurfer's paradise. Strolling along the beaches of modern-day Essaouira, feeling the strong winds, listening to the pounding surf, one can readily imagine ancient ships anchored offshore. Past the fortified walls

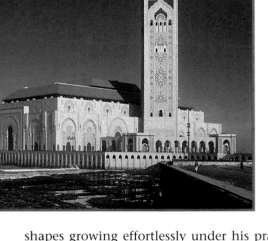

surrounding the small town, squares empty into narrow lanes. Loosely woven reed mats hang overhead, diffusing the bright sunshine and casting shadows on the walls. Whitewashed houses with brightly painted doors are home to local artisans engaged in the age-old craft of woodworking. The sound of rasping handsaws and clinking hammers accompanies the sharp fragrance of fresh thuya wood hanging in the air. Men and boys hover in shaded cubicles, expertly fashioning trunks and beds, chairs and boxes, statues and toys. An artisan patiently inlays a geometric design on a tabletop, the shapes growing effortlessly under his practiced hands. These handcrafted tables—all made in Essaouira—can be found throughout Morocco.

In the southern Sous region, named for the Sous River near Agadir, along the spectacular Atlantic coast, the scenery alternates between rugged, rocky stretches and wide, serene

The Grand Mosque of Casablanca, Mosque Hassan II, was opened to worshippers in 1993, after thirteen years of construction. Its foundation was anchored to rocks reclaimed from the ocean, and its six-hundred-foot (183m)-high minaret is visible from miles away. The mosque is second in size only to the grand mosque in Mecca; St. Peter's Basilica would easily fit inside it.

beaches modulated by sandy dunes. The towns along the coast are far enough apart to create pockets of near isolation. For miles, beachcombers can listen to and watch the ceaseless motion of waves against the backdrop of an endlessly blue sky.

The coast becomes more lively in and around the active city of Agadir. The bustle of an animated seaside resort fills the air, and the scent of suntan oil mingles with fresh ocean breezes. Children build sandcastles while the local teenagers play soccer. Crowds of umbrellas and lounge chairs give way to rarified enclaves of private beaches occupied by sun-loving foreign visitors. Luxurious resorts and charming hotels abound. Restaurants catering to international tastes serve locally caught seafood on linen-covered tables. This, too, is Morocco, an aspect of the country that offers a glimpse of how effortlessly Moroccans have merged tourism with history, turning this seventeenth-century seaport into a thriving travel center.

Yet, to this day, fishing remains an important local industry. On the northern outskirts of town, near the harbor, an active fish market supplies local restaurants and merchants.

Agadir is far enough south to offer sunshine year-round— and rain showers are few and far between. Date palms grace gardens and streets, and the sweet scent of night jasmine perfumes the air. Bright magenta bougainvillea sprawls over walls in lavish profusion. Cacti grow forbidding thorns, signaling the town's proximity to ever-encroaching desert. Following the contours of the sand dunes southward, just a short walk along the water's edge, Sous-Massa National Park is home to hundreds of species of migrating birds. The most spectacular sight along the fertile riverbanks of the park are the great pink flamingos. Stealthily tiptoeing on their pencil-thin legs, or precariously balancing their rosy-feathered bodies on one leg, flocks of these birds arrive from Spain to spend the winter here.

The sardine fishermen of Essaouira have spread their many-hued fishing nets on the shores of this historic seaside town for three centuries. Historically known to sailors and traders as Mogador, the windswept beaches of Essaouira are now shared with surfers who come from all over the world to enjoy the waves.

The Mountains

In all the magnificence of the geographic diversity of Morocco, there is no match for the visual impact of the Atlas Mountains. There dwelt Atlas, who, according to Greek mythology, was a Titan who joined with his brother, Cronus, to fight the Olympians. Defeated, Atlas was condemned by Zeus to the eternal labor of bearing the earth and the heavens upon his shoulders. In Arabic, the mountains are Jezira el-Machreb, "Island of the West," because the range is an "island" of fertility in an arid land.

Stretching almost the entire width of the country, the three Atlas ranges—High, Middle, and Anti Atlas—are the most prominent features of Morocco's landscape. The snow-covered peaks of the High Atlas soar to more than thirteen thousand feet (4,000m). Winters are bitterly cold. Even at lower elevations, snowfalls start in October and make roads impassable until March. Weather conditions and terrain keep villages and valleys isolated from one another. Starting in the southern Anti-Atlas range, a simple country road, or *piste*, winds slowly higher around arid, brown hills. The landscape becomes inhospitable; steep, rocky mountains loom beyond and extend toward the horizon. Shriveled trees and bushes provide meager nourishment for grazing goats.

So far south, the desert is close. Habitation is possible only where water can be found. Driving mile after mile, the road hardly wider than a single lane, not a soul is in sight. Then, perfectly camouflaged, buildings can suddenly be discerned on a distant mountaintop. On closer approach, an ancient casbah rises up. Cubelike houses seem to grow organically out of the countryside, built here of stone rather than mud, as is typical deeper inland. Strong walls surround the foot of the buildings, forming a fortress-like enclosure. Homes are stacked over and into each other, the flat roof of one house forming the balcony of another. Nearby, terraces are carefully maintained amidst the rocks, taking advantage of scarce farmland in this forbidding landscape. For generations, these plots have been planted and irrigated, sharing precious water in a spirit of kinship. After the harvest, they blend back

The "Mountain of Mountains," Jebel Toubkal is the highest in North Africa (13,661 feet [4,164m]). As the crow flies, it is a mere fifty miles (80km) south of Marrakech. Imagine the unfolding of mountainscapes as the city is left behind and the snowy peaks of the Toubkal Massif come within reach.

into the rest of the mountains, brown and dry until the next growing season.

As one winds farther through the Anti-Atlas, casbahs appear more frequently. The gently rolling lower mountain ranges are more expansive, reaching toward sections of wild stone formations. The tints of the landscape change as well—shades of earthy brown give way to rich reddish-rusty hues, while hills in the distance look vaguely purple. Finally, the first sighting of greenery and water-enriched life appears in a valley sloping down from the road. Fed by an abundant underground water supply, the oasis is a feast for the eyes: little boys tend their goats under date palms heavy with fruit and, high atop a tower, a large bird's nest perches—home to one of many stork families in Morocco.

Most towns in these mountains are little more than a cluster of homes along a main road. The buildings are hugged by impressive, intensely copper-colored rock formations. Smooth, rounded boulders are strewn through the landscape like the remnants of a game among long-vanished Titans. Women, shrouded in black from head to toe, walk through town; a few men sit and smoke in front of a small general store. Overlooking the valley is a hotel catering to vacationers. A noticeable stillness permeates this remote place—travelers are likely to spend little more than lunchtime here. That, however, is regrettable, because out-of-the way places often harbor unexpected gems.

One such treasure might be a rug trader's shop, offering carpets and *kilims* that are hooked and woven in neighboring valleys. The traditional weavings of the Berber tribes dominate, though rugs in the "Oriental" style may also be found.

Intricate diamond shapes, stars, and zigzag lines in saffron yellows and pepper reds alternate with black and white. Bold geometric patterns are intercepted by stripes in rich earthy tones of ochre and brown. The colors borrow the hues of the nearby countryside, of the sun dipping over boulders and painting them shades of glowing orange. A weaver's loom catches breezy blues and untouched whites, like puffy clouds on azure sky. Threads like rays of golden light weave in and out of patterns. Wool and cotton are the medium for the women who design these collectibles—they are artists who amaze with the magnitude of their imaginations. Inspired by the timelessness of their stony surroundings, their creativity flourishing in this harsh, craggy environment, the weavers invent complex designs, so fine and delicate that they call to mind the intricate beauty of filigree jewelry. Each carpet is exquisite, nurturing a pervasive desire simply to sit quietly and allow these marvels to impress themselves on mind and soul.

The mountains have been inhabited longer than any other region of Morocco. As early as the Bronze Age, humans left carvings and paintings telling of the animals and people who roamed here. Then, some four thousand years ago, the people now known as Berbers came to settle. Nobody knows with any degree of certainty where they came from, although it has been claimed that they migrated from Central Asia, perhaps Kazakhstan. Berber myths speak of worshipping the sun and sacrificing to the moon, millennia before the advent of Islam. Yet the Berber people have no written history; their regional dialects, traditions, and crafts are passed on from parent to child.

Close to half the population of Morocco is of Berber descent. Traditional Berbers call themselves *Shloh*, meaning noble, or more commonly *Imazhigen*, or Free People—telling descriptions for these dignified and straightforward men and women who stand tall both in stature and in character. Throughout their long history, they have been known as rebels who refuse subjugation. From shops in cities to small settlements in remote corners of the country, their dialects are heard everywhere. Because family and custom are such integral parts of a Berber's life, they prefer living as close-knit tribes, inhabiting the various regions of the Atlas. The clan names by which they identify themselves tell of their native lands. *Ait* means "people of," and so we find the Ait Mizane, Ait Atta, Ait Haddidou, and many more.

Some Berbers, like the Ait Atta, are self-sufficient nomads who roam the High Atlas in the summer months, spending the winters in the plains and valleys. A family's belongings fit easily on the back of a single mule. Living in low, dark brown tents visible from afar, they keep their goats, sheep, and mules nearby, tending to the needs of their flock before their own needs. Amidst spectacular scenery, their quiet life is disturbed only by the howling of jackals and the sound of the winds tugging on their tents.

Berber women have a reputation for fierce independence. They tattoo their chins from the lips down the center in designs of stripes, dots, and zigzags, rubbing indigo or gunpowder into the skin. The older they are, the more elaborate the tattoo is likely to be. Their brightly colored dresses are often covered by roughly woven striped shawls for warmth. Triangular silver brooches, ornamented with wire and colored glass, pin their draping clothes together. Their jewelry is bold and heavy; they gracefully wear thick necklaces adorned with bright red coral or amber beads the size of chestnuts, and wide silver bracelets weigh down both wrists. Ornamental chains, often with antique coins attached to them, hang on their headscarves. Berber women do not hide their

Peeking from behind the warp of a rug she is knotting, this Berber woman near Imilchil takes a break from her labors. The design and color combinations used in the rug will identify the tribe and region in which a kilim was made.

faces behind veils. They are free to choose their husbands for themselves, and they may divorce just as easily.

These ways and others are celebrated in many Berber festivals known as *moussems*, which are common during the summer months. Held to honor local saints, or *marabouts*, moussems often combine tribal traditions, Islamic customs, and a market for goods and jewelry. Moreover, news and gossip are exchanged when friends and families gather together at these festive events.

In Imilchil in the High Atlas, the Berber tribe Ait Haddidou plans their three-day moussem according to the moon; if it is not a full moon by the intended date, the festival is delayed until the most auspicious day. This moussem is the *Fête des Fiancés*, also known as the "Marriage Market," a means of securing the future of their clan. Each year in late September, the tribe gathers in this remote mountain village. It is at this gathering that the women choose husbands. Their headdresses identify them as divorced or as never married: the divorced women wear a pointed hood, whereas a scarf wrapped tight and flat around the head indicates a woman searching for her first husband. Much dancing and singing accompanies this moussem as the women wander among the tents in hopes of finding a husband. Should a couple agree to a union, a notary is called to register the intent of bride and groom—the actual marriage ceremony will not take place until after the harvest. On the day of the wedding, the extended family will be entertained with traditional food and music. The new bride then rides to the groom's house, where her husband's mother will carry her over the threshold.

Marrakech and the Souks

West of the Atlas Mountains and their magnificent passes, in the midst of a fertile plain, the "Red City" of Marrakech appears like a fairy tale. The Koutoubia Mosque, with its towering minaret, greets approaching travelers from miles away.

Founded in the year 1062 by the Almoravid sultan Youssef bin Tachfin, Marrakech quickly became the gem of Morocco. As the Almoravids extended their control of Morocco and Spain, they also developed the city's infrastructure and architecture—it was Youssef bin Tachfin's successor and son, Ali, who ordered the construction of the Marrakech *khettara*, an underground irrigation system that continues to provide the city's many gardens with water today. The riches that flowed in from the conquest of Spain were used to beautify the city; craftsmen imported from Moorish Spain built palaces, baths, and mosques.

Surrounding the medina to this day are red earth walls built in 1126. Legend has it that they gained their distinctive hue from the blood that flowed from the Koutoubia Mosque—the rays of the setting sun paint the walls a glowing shade of crimson, earning Marrakech its reputation as the Red City.

But it was the "Golden Sultan," Ahmed al-Mansour—ruler of the Saadian dynasty until 1603—who built the beautiful Palais el-Badi. Known at the time as "the Incomparable," the el-Badi Palace is a wonder of artistry and construction, built with precious materials imported from far and wide and financed primarily by the spoils of victory over the Portuguese at the

Battle of the Three Kings in 1578. The Palais el-Badi is now mostly in ruins, but some of its former splendor can still be explored. Sunken gardens and pools intended to cool the air dot the grounds, and the ruins of the Koubba al-Khamsiniyya, a great hall used for state receptions, offer a glimpse of the palace's former glory.

Better preserved is another one of al-Mansour's projects, the long-secret Saadian Tombs, built in the late 1500s. Although other great constructions of the day were razed and ravaged during the seventeenth century, this ancient necropolis was instead sealed (perhaps because of superstitions about disturbing the dead) and essentially forgotten. It was not until the early 1900s that the tombs were reopened and restored, and with most of their contents—including the remains of al-Mansour and his family—undisturbed, the Saadian Tombs provide a look at the opulence of a long gone era.

Over the following centuries, several other dynasties ruled and expanded the city. Although it remained an imperial city and was home to numerous sultans, the rivaling cities of Fez and Meknès, favored by the Merinide rulers, gained in importance while Marrakech declined. From French colonial times until independence in 1956, Marrakech's past grandeur returned with Pasha el-Glaoui, a man famous for his lavish lifestyle and parties that lasted for days. The Glaoui family's rise to power reads like an adventure novel: they once were simple clan leaders who controlled an important caravan route between Marrakech and the valleys of the Draa and Dades rivers. In 1893, they shrewdly aided Sultan Mulay Hassan after an unsuccessful burning raid. For this, they were rewarded with administrative supervision of the entire region between the High Atlas and the Sahara. By the time the French arrived in Morocco in 1912, the Glaoui were firmly in power. They pledged allegiance to the French, who in turn made them pashas of Marrakech. Regarded by many Berber tribes as traitors to a foreign power for their own aggrandizement, Glaoui lived in a style that became legend. When el-Glaoui was literally on his deathbed in 1956, a mob assembled. As soon as his death was announced, the murder of his henchmen and the looting and destruction of his palace brought this era to an end.

The heart of today's Marrakech can be found in its souks and in its lively central square, the Djemaa el-Fna. Small towns may have a market day once a week, attracting shoppers from the entire region. These markets often focus on produce and everyday household items: fresh eggs balance atop each other precariously; tables filled with mounds of spices perch near displays of ropes and reed mats. The scent of freshly cut mint, an essential ingredient in sweet mint tea, wafts through the air. In contrast to the small town market stalls, however, the souks of Marrakech are a world of their own. Fascinatingly colorful, the shops are strung along the winding streets of the old medina. The maze of souks has the ambience of times gone by, enchanting and disarming like a spell. Author and playwright Elias Canetti observed:

> *It is spicy in the souks, and cool and colorful. The smell, always pleasant, changes gradually with the nature of the merchandise. There are no names or signs, there is no glass. . . . You find everything—but you find it many times over.*

These old lanes have seen the same turbaned men, wearing the same style of slippers, speaking the same dialects, for centuries. Little has changed here; artisans still work in the shadowy cubicles of their respective quarters, using tools and techniques that have been handed down from generation to generation. The goods are stacked and presented in customary ways, separated by craft— leather with leather, brass with brass, wood with wood. The coppersmiths are far away from the apothecary stalls, the carpenters distanced from the carpet sellers. Gold and silver, clothing and baskets, rugs and spices are kept apart, according to mystical rules that established their distance from each other long ago, and that have been observed religiously for centuries since.

Along the Souk of the Slippermakers, thirty or forty stalls sell the same soft Moroccan slippers, called *babouches*. They come in tan, red, and yellow; they may be plain or embroidered, but all are neatly arranged, row after row, with the shopkeeper sitting cross-legged among or behind the slippers like an overseer of shoes. Not a single item is marked with a price tag, leaving shoppers to grapple with the great mystery of souks: how much to pay, and where to buy when all stalls offer the same merchandise? The merchant may appear nonchalant and distant, but even the slightest interest in anything he has to offer begins the great ritual of testing and charming, appraising and cajoling. A mere hesitation by the passerby, a moment when the eyes rest on something, and this classic Moroccan ritual commences.

The bargaining is not an attempt to be difficult or to confuse the outsider. It is a tradition, a ceremony, and even a form of entertainment, without which the shopkeeper feels almost shortchanged and certainly deprived of the pleasure of the game of buying and selling. Time is of no consequence. The customer, invited to rest and share refreshments, is honored with hospitality and conversation. At a moment's notice, a boy appears bearing a tray of glasses and a small pot of fragrant mint tea. It will serve the buyer well to open

Carpets are always a visual delight, their harmonious symmetry offering a startling counterpoint to the wild, untamed countryside in which they are made. Knotted or woven by women in the tranquillity of the mountains, the carpets incorporate the bright, earthy shades of their native land.

up a bit, to return the hospitality of the shopkeeper with courtesy. This is a meeting of sorts—an exchange that goes deeper than simply bargaining for goods. In the discussing, people get together, sharing stories of their worlds. News travels this way, and gossip, but mainly this ceremony allows people of different cultures to connect. After the initial connection is made the bargaining can begin in earnest. A price will be mentioned; never should this first price be accepted without politely reducing it, and neither side should appear too eager to make a deal. The process is like a dance, with the buyer leading one moment and the seller the next, each side using a unique combination of charm, subtle pressure, and disarming arguments. It serves the buyer well to be as talkative as the seller, for it is the greatest compliment to be told that one haggles "like a Berber." In most cases, the

merchandise eventually changes hands, perhaps at a price that is still too high, but this will always remain the secret of the souk.

As one leaves the sheltered lanes of the souk behind, the Djemaa el-Fna rises ahead like a medieval public theater. The most exotic place of amusement in all of Morocco, the square is a sight to see at any time of day, but in the late afternoon and early evening it truly comes to life. Located in the heart of the medina, its name means "Assembly of the Dead," a reference to the square's history of hosting public executions and displaying criminals' heads as recently as the late nineteenth century. Colorfully clad water-sellers with wide-brimmed straw hats and brightly polished brass cups pose for pictures while Berber dancers call attention away from musicians who play native tunes on their exotic instruments.

It sparkles and it shines in the Souk of the Coppersmiths in Marrakech. A large part of the market is devoted to their craft. Their wares are bent, hammered, and shaped with techniques that have been used for many centuries.

As darkness falls, hissing hurricane lamps cast flickering shadows on the dense crowds packing the square. Baskets full of freshly baked flat bread surround a row of women. Sometimes one of them will pick up a loaf and tap its bottom while offering it for sale to passersby. Not far away, food is prepared and served along rows of tables and benches. Dark red beets, cooked and sliced, fill a large bowl. Grated carrots flavored with orange juice fill another. Skewers with charbroiled pieces of meat are stacked on a grill, where they are busily turned by the cook. Fragrant stews—a mix of potatoes, pumpkin, tomatoes, onions, peas, and meat, garnished with olives and chunks of lemon—sit in shallow earthenware pots with cone-shaped lids to keep the heat in. This is the classic *tajine* of Morocco. Spiced with turmeric, red pepper, and saffron, it is not eaten with utensils, but with chunks of bread which are used to scoop and soak up the stew. Another specialty is the small hills

of steaming, light couscous—sometimes set up in tureens with cinnamon and sugar sprinkled over it, but more often served with steamed and spiced vegetables. For dessert, orange slices with a dusting of cinnamon swim in their natural juice. Patrons order their selections buffet-style and enjoy them outdoors in the tarp-covered eatery.

Elsewhere in the Djemaa, wiry acrobats as flexible as rubber show off their skills, contorting their bodies and somersaulting through the air. A dentist sits cross-legged on a mat, his instruments neatly arranged around him (along with spare dentures and individual teeth in various sizes), patiently waiting for customers. The largest crowd encircles the storyteller, listening attentively to his tales with appreciative smiles on their faces. Storytelling is a tradition in Morocco, the familiar tales savored in the recounting. The magician on his flying carpet cast his spells from here, the *Maghreb*, the Land of the West.

At the heart of Marrakech, in the Djemaa el-Fna, a feast for all the senses, heady and subtle. And threading through the marketplace, the sweet ubiquitous scent of mint tea.

Nearby, a snake charmer is preparing to open a wooden box to allow a cobra to escape the darkness of its prison. Flute in hand, he slides the lid off the box and shakes it a little to encourage the snake to hurry. Head first, a cobra emerges and begins to slither away from its master. As the audience nervously scrambles out of the snake's way, the snake charmer takes a few big steps, bends down, and grabs the snake by its tail, pulling it back into the circle. Noticeably relieved, the crowd watches as the charmer begins playing his flute, and the snake responds—it is not clear if the snake is hypnotized by the tune or by the charmer, who sways his body slightly. One wonders who is dancing for whom; both appear equally spellbound by the other.

Fez

Early in the morning, long before the first light of day breaks the velvety darkness of night, stillness envelops homes and tiptoes delicately along the cobbled lanes of the city. The silvery sliver of a new moon casts a pale glow on glazed tile. A faint breeze, hardly detectable, rustles the leaves of a branch hanging languidly over a wall. The heady fragrance of sweet jasmine wafts across a courtyard, above a fountain's basin filled with water.

A steady, calm note breaks the silence of night. A sound hovering in midair, originating from above the roofs, becomes a word, a chant. *"All—ah—Ak—bar"* (God is great) fills the night and grows louder, more persistent. The *muezzin* is calling the faithful to morning prayer. From the minaret, a song floats over the city, rousing man, woman, and child from

sleep. Soft slippers flip-flop over stone, as someone hurries through the predawn stillness to the nearby mosque for ablution and prayer. Presently, from a slightly different direction, another call to prayer arises. Then a third joins in, filling the air with its song. As the chants overlap and intensify, roosters stir in backyards and add their secular wake-up call to the music of the muezzin. Soon the air is filled with different calls to prayer from all over the city; the sounds fuse and transform into waves rolling over the rooftops, finally metamorphosing into a monotone hum, a reverberation so intense it is felt deep within the body.

There is an old Fassi saying: "All roads in Fez lead to the Kairouine Mosque." Although this may not literally be the case, what becomes most obvious to the visitor is that all roads lead to a mosque. Fez, historically the religious and cultural center of Morocco, is studded with these jewels of medieval architecture. It has been suggested that Fez el-Bali, the old town founded by Moulay Idriss II around the year 800 C.E., is home to hundreds of mosques.

Although its beginnings were modest, Fez started its expansion with the arrival of thousands of families from Moorish Andalusia. Later, emigrants from Kairouan, Tunisia, an important center of Muslim learning, joined these families. The cultural and religious legacy of these people, as well as their architectural heritage, laid the foundation for Fez to become a hub of religious studies. During the reign of the Merenids, this base was greatly expanded by the development of the new city of Fez el-Djedid alongside the old medina of Fez el-Bali. The Kairouine Mosque was built in the 1300s;

Between doors of carved cedar, a glimpse into one of Fez's medieval *medersas*, or places of study. Medersas are colleges and dormitories, with prayer halls for devotional services, which have flourished in Fez from the thirteenth century on. Several have been restored in recent years and are still in use today, offering teachings in theology, law, and Arabic.

Kairouine University saw the addition of *medersas*, college housing for students who came from the farthest corners of the Muslim world to study.

The magnificent architecture of the Kairouine Mosque, large enough to accommodate twenty thousand people, inspires admiration, even awe in the visitor. Walking on this quarter's narrow cobblestones, one is astounded by the beauty of the medieval craftsmanship. Arabesques of colorful tiles and intricacies of beautifully preserved cedar-wood carvings over doorways blend into a dazzling array of shape and design. An open passage into the mosque leads to a farther gate and corridor into a cavernous, cool hall. Oversized carved doors open to immense rooms; the wood is a display of intertwined squares and stars, where latticed sections let light and air circulate. The natural hue of the wood calms and at the same time enhances the dizzying detail of sky blue and gold tile on white background. Intricate calligraphy winds throughout the design, with vines and repetitive geometric patterns constantly reappearing. Arabesques carved in stucco and plaster are as fine and delicate as jewelwork, their simple ivory color pristine against the weight of a solid, carved overhang, or a pillar tiled from bottom to top.

Friday morning is a good time to explore Fez and have it almost to oneself. This being their Sabbath, the inhabitants of the city, the Fassi, are taking time off, and the fortress-like walls and narrow, winding alleys are quiet and shady. It is an adventure to make one's way between walls without windows rising up on both sides, so high that sunlight can barely penetrate to street level. Sometimes, outstretched arms can easily touch both sides of the passageway. At other spots, the lanes are wide enough to allow a donkey, the common beast of burden, to pass through with a bulky bundle tied to its back. Fez's medina is confusing, and finding one's way can seem like a game of hide-and-seek. Twists and turns materialize out of nowhere, and orientation is confused by the illusory similarity of one street to the next. A road might dead-end here, or open onto a small neighborhood square there, where a lonely tree is the sole greenery amid historic architecture. Water fountains used for hundreds of years provide landmarks by which to set one's compass. The *hammam,* or bath, segregated by gender, has been an integral part of each quarter for centuries, as has the public bakery, essentially a large wood-burning stove in a part of a building, to which the neighborhood women bring loaves of dough on large trays to have them baked.

Wandering through this ancient city, touching a stonemason's work from the Middle Ages or sailing along the shores plied by seafarers and spice traders of thousands of years ago, history comes to life, and ages past feel almost within reach.

OPPOSITE: **More than in any other Moroccan city, the use of wood in architecture reached a high level of development in Fez. Used for structural as well as decorative purposes, cedar carvings and painted wood are found throughout Old Fez. Here,** *zouak***—the traditional technique of painting on wood—decorates an ornate doorway at the National Museum in Fez.**

PART 2

IMAGES

PAGES 30–31: **The sand dunes of Merzouga, the *Erg Chebbi*, have long fascinated all those who encounter them: photographers and artists have tried to capture the perpetual transformation of the landscape on film and in words. These are the largest sand dunes in Morocco, and nature lovers marvel at the amazing adaptability of flora and fauna to a seemingly inhospitable environment.**

ABOVE: **Ait Ben Haddou looks as if Hollywood had it made to order. It is more elaborately decorated than many casbahs—with geometrical shapes carved into walls and a multitude of small openings serving as windows—and spacious enough for people, food, supplies, and livestock.**

RIGHT: **These Gnaoua singers are members of an ancient brotherhood. Distant descendants of Sub-Saharan slaves, they give evidence of the movement of people from the Sahara, Mauritania, and the ancient kingdom of Timbuktu.**

ABOVE: **A fine example of Islamic art, the Ambassador's Gateway in the Royal Palace in Rabat displays multihued, geometrical patterns of inlaid tile. The *zelliges* in turn, are framed by intricate and gilded sculpted plaster called *tagguebbast*. Always abstract, the designs are meant to draw attention away from daily life into a world of pure ordered form.**

OPPOSITE: **Mirroring the reddish rocks and sandy earth of the surrounding terrain, this casbah in the hot southeastern interior, near Al-Rachidia, incorporates the architectural style and materials that have been used in this region for ages. These Berber palaces, their earthen walls baked by the fierce sun, their window bordered with lime, will fall into disrepair if not continuously maintained.**

LEFT: **Al-Jadida, called Mazagan by the founding Portuguese between 1562 and 1769, is home to this Portuguese cistern. Now used as a water-storage facility, it was originally designed to store munitions. Sunlight coming from a single opening reflects over the water and casts an enchanting glow over five rows of columns supporting the structure. Though more than 1,300 square yards (1,189m²) in size, this crypt-like cistern was lost for 150 years, only to be rediscovered under the current medina in 1916.**

ABOVE: **Berber pottery is both functional and simple. Jugs like these have been made on potter's wheels for centuries. The clay is fired at low temperatures and is unglazed; this allows for a modest surface evaporation, thereby keeping the liquid stored inside naturally cool.**

ABOVE: **Traditionally, bread is not simply part of each meal, it is used instead of fork or spoon: by holding a piece of bread with three fingers of the right hand, food is taken from the communal bowl, and juices of native dishes like** *tajine* **are soaked up.**

OPPOSITE: **Whitewashed and pristine, the town of Chaouen, deep in the rugged Rif Mountains, invites a walking tour through its twisting lanes. The laid-back, relaxing atmosphere has not changed much even with recent growth. Located far enough from both Tangier and Tétouan, Chaouen exudes a sense of quiet Rif life.**

OPPOSITE: **The snow-covered Atlas Mountains stand cool, with the air of eternity, against the tropical nonchalance of a date palm. Often separated by only a hundred miles, the difference in elevation creates avalanches in the mountains, while orchards bask in the hot sun.**

RIGHT: **The Erg Chebbi sand dunes are among the most stunning sights in Morocco. One of the few tribes that have adapted to the harsh desert environment is the Tuareg— colloquially called "the blue people." They received their name because of the blue cloth they use for their flowing robes, the dye from which leaves a bluish tint on the skin.**

So typical of Islamic architecture—and so enchanting to the Western eye—are the many arches throughout Moroccan buildings. In mosques, palaces, and homes, arcades like this one uniquely blend load-bearing structural elements and ornamental forms.

OPPOSITE: **Volubilis, just east of modern-day Rabat, was already the western capital of a Berber kingdom before it was annexed by the Roman Empire in 45 C.E. Sprawling over 100 acres (40 ha), the well-maintained ruins we see today date mainly from the second and third centuries. Exquisitely detailed mosaics are found in the House of the Beasts, the House of the Labors of Hercules, and the House of Orpheus.**

ABOVE: **Near Rabat's twelfth-century Tower of Hassan is the Mausoleum of King Mohammed V, who is known as the Father of Independence. A masterpiece of classical Moroccan architecture, the tower was completed in 1971, and contains within its walls a mosque, a small museum, arcades, and the sarcophagus of Mohammed V.**

LEFT: **The Draa Valley is home to a number of casbahs,
none more spectacular than the Ksour at Tamnougalt.
Set against a rugged mountain backdrop, this rambling
complex is home to the Mezguita tribe.**

ABOVE: **Typical of the earth tones and organic forms
in the deep southeast, this gate can be found within the
ancient casbah of Al-Rachidia. Also called Ksar-Es-Souk,
this palm grove town is a rest stop on the
South Atlas Highway to Algeria.**

OPPOSITE: **Mounds of steaming couscous beckon hungry visitors in Marrakech's Djemaa el-Fna. At sundown,
the square fills with people who stop by to have their evening meal after work, as well as tourists
who are tempted by the fragrant scents of paprika-flavored tajines.**

ABOVE: **Flocks of sheep dot the countryside, grazing on pristine meadows in the Atlas Mountains.
To mark the end of Ramadan, the month of fasting, and to celebrate special holidays, they are brought to market.
Every family that can afford a sheep will buy one for the feast.**

OPPOSITE: Europeans have called the camel "the ship of the desert," but the relationship between the people of Africa and their beasts of burden is an agelessly intimate one.

ABOVE: There is nothing more delightful, nothing more colorful than springtime's abundance of wildflowers on mountain meadows. Letting his herd graze on the fields beyond, a shepherd chats with a passing farmer.

OPPOSITE: **A man in his striped djellaba, the scorched desert plain against a deeply blue sky, and the simple structure of a marabout's tomb. The domed tombs of these local saints dot the countryside and are believed to offer blessings and the saint's protection; they are popular places of worship and pilgrimage.**

ABOVE: **The southern Dades Valley is arid and barren, save for the oases, lush and green against the inhospitable hills. Even here, numerous casbahs are scattered throughout the region. Most, like the casbah at Ait Oudinar, were built rather recently—in the nineteenth century.**

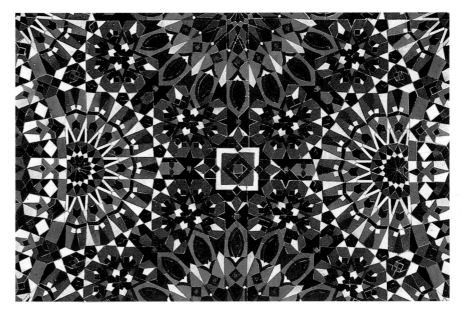

LEFT: **Basins of water are always a great luxury and sign of wealth in the hot desert. With scorching summer temperatures, it is rejuvenating to spend some time by the Saadian Pavilion and the refreshing pool of the Menara Gardens of Marrakech. An intricate system of underground channels feeds the twelfth-century central pool and provides irrigation to the surrounding olive groves.**

ABOVE: **Intricate detail and repetition of form create this kaleidoscope of mosaic tile in Casablanca's Hassan II Mosque. Depicting life forms is forbidden in Islam, so craftsmen and master tile layers have elevated geometric ornamentation into an artform.**

OPPOSITE: **A barley field near Taroudant is sprinkled with poppies and daisies. This gateway to the Anti-Atlas region just east of Agadir is the ancient capital of the Sous region. Its history begins in 1056, when the Almoravids conquered the city; over the centuries, different dynasties maintained their rule within the mud walls that surround the town.**

ABOVE: **Bobbins of silk thread in a tailor's shop. Predominantly men to this day, tailors are employed even in the smallest villages to sew clothes, but also household items like cushions and bedspreads. Though sewing machines have become common, much is still stitched by hand.**

PAGES 58–59: **A whimsical view of the minaret of the Hassan II Mosque in Casablanca, which towers over the enormous mosque. At 562 feet (171m), it is the tallest minaret in the world. Throughout its thirteen-year construction, the craftsmen utilized all Moroccan materials, with the exception of glass imported from Italy. The mosque complex will eventually include a museum, library, and a medersa.**

ABOVE: **The richly ornamental tiles called *zelliges* create hypnotic patterns on interior walls in homes and mosques. Geometric principles of symmetry and repetition are often complemented by the serpentine spirals of arabesques.**

RIGHT: **Rays of sunshine reflect off the copper and brass merchandise on display in the Souk of the Coppersmiths. Trays, mirrors, teapots, and cauldrons are stacked in front of the shop, and from floor to ceiling inside. Pieces are either hammered or chased copper and brass, with designs chiseled into metal by artisans in nearby workshops.**

Glazed pots in designs and shapes typical of the potters of Fez are displayed in an antique shop.
Though an intense blue is the most common color for Fassi pottery, the green and yellow pattern often characterizes
the covered jars called *jobbana*, which were once used to store cheese. These late-nineteenth-century originals
find their modern counterparts still bearing traditional patterns.

Colorful yarn draped over bamboo racks dries in the heat of the sun in the Dyers' Souk. Yarn is hand-dipped into cauldrons filled with dye, and dye workers' bare arms and legs clearly give away their occupation. From the tenth to the nineteenth century, the dyers and tanners of Fez maintained the commercial wealth of the city.

ABOVE: **Fez has long been known as a leather-making center. The first requirement for this trade is a reliable source of fresh water, and the city's location on the Sebou River assures the tanners of a steady supply. The stone vats, the manual labor, and the techniques have remained the same for centuries.**

RIGHT: **The pungent smell of the tanneries emanates from these hides drying in the sun. Fez has a large Tanners' Souk, in which leather is treated and dyed using traditional methods. The leather produced is prized the world over for its softness and suppleness.**

ABOVE: **Traditional shades of blue—from aqua to turquoise to navy—form a frame around the mosaic zelliges of a mosque doorway in the small holy town of Chaouen, in the northern Rif Mountains.**

RIGHT: **The ramparts of Essaouira tell of an era when this small fishing village on the Atlantic was a daunting fortress. Raised originally by the Portuguese in the sixteenth century, most of the massive walls around the town were built under the reign of the Berber sultan Sidi Mohammed bin Adballah, who took over the city in 1765.**

ABOVE: From the fifteenth century on, the seafaring Portuguese were a presence along the coastline of Morocco, establishing trading posts and forts from Tangier to Agadir. Before them and after them, Moroccan fishermen plied the same waters; today, the fishing industry makes substantial contributions to the economy.

OPPOSITE: The influence of southern European architecture on the Moroccan cities across the Strait of Gibraltar is apparent here. Wooden window shutters and an ornate lamp are reminiscent of Spanish homes. Small windows serve a dual function: they preserve privacy while keeping the summer heat at bay.

The small regional center of Tinherir is
a base for excursions to the Todra
Gorge, the Grand Canyon of Morocco.
Once home to a garrison of the French
Foreign Legion, it is a quiet hamlet
built above an oasis of palm groves
and olive and walnut trees. Like all
mud-brick buildings that are not
constantly maintained, this casbah
has fallen into disrepair, even ruin.

ABOVE: **The use of bold red creates a stark contrast with the blue door of an inner courtyard. Blue of any shade is a popular color for the wooden or metal doors of houses, as it is believed to repel flies and other insects.**

OPPOSITE: **The juxtaposition of radiant shades has always been part of Morocco's allure for painters from Eugène Delacroix to Henri Matisse. For centuries, it has inspired artists to play with the bold contrasts visible in the most ordinary places.**

ABOVE: **Brightly glazed green tile roofs are seen in cities throughout the country. In medieval times,**
green tile was used exclusively in the construction of religious and royal buildings,
green being the sacred color of Islam.

OPPOSITE: **Hassan Tower in Rabat is the minaret and the only completed building of an enormous mosque**
project started by the Almohad sultan Yakoub al-Mansour in 1195. The 360 pillars arranged around
the tower were intended to support the roof of the mosque, but construction was
abandoned with the sultan's early death in 1199.

LEFT: **Sitting on a doorstep in quiet conversation, these men wait out the rain. The bright turquoise color of the door is popular in northern Morocco, where it reflects the azure skies above and makes the white plastered walls look even brighter.**

OPPOSITE: **Carefully cultivated fields and groves are signs of water. Although the Draa nourishes the fields along its course, winter rains only rarely swell the river enough to allow it to reach the ocean.**

ABOVE: Taroudant is the ancient capital of the Sous Valley in the south of
Morocco. Adobe walls more than three miles (4.8km) long and about
eighteen feet (5.5m) high have enclosed the town since they were built in
the 1700s. A walk or drive at sunset, when the walls are cast in a warm,
rusty-reddish glow, is especially memorable.

RIGHT: Around 1150, Abd al-Moumen, first sultan of the Almohad dynasty,
erected a casbah on the site of a seventh-century fortified monastery.
This *ribat* on the mouth of the Bu Regreg was further expanded by
his grandson Yacoub al-Mansour. Al-Mansour added several miles of walls
around the casbah during an ambitious building phase that included the ancient
Hassan Tower, still standing in the sophisticated capital today called Rabat.

OPPOSITE: **The fountain's basin, once used for ritual washing, is the focal point of this medieval medersa in Fez. All around are classical decorative elements, forming a harmonious whole, from intricate zellige designs, to arches richly carved of plaster or cedar wood.**

RIGHT: **The Royal Palace's gates in Fez are among the finest examples of craftsmanship to be found in Morocco. The brass doors, representing the official entrance to the palace, are traditionally used by the king and his guests during ceremonial occasions. Behind these gates are various palaces and pavilions spread over 160 acres (64 ha).**

A woman hurrying along the street almost looks like an apparition, her white garments blending into the whitewashed mud wall. The anonymous building and the shrouded woman emanate a sense of secrecy, so typical throughout a country where people jealously guard their privacy.

With lanes barely wide enough for two men to walk shoulder to shoulder, the blue and whitewashed walls of adjacent houses seem to create a labyrinth. With so many twists and turns, often with no street signs, navigation can be difficult for the uninitiated.

OPPOSITE: The star-shaped fountain in front of the Hassan II Mosque in Casablanca is a beautiful example of artisanal work. Broken pieces of tile are arranged in repetitive geometric patterns over the entire surface, while ripples on the shallow water continually vary the effect of the vividly colored, inlaid arabesques on the bottom of the basin.

RIGHT: Four major gates in the ancient city wall lead into Old Fez, one at each of the cardinal points. Bab Bou Jeloud, the Western Gate, is the most ornate and, with its handsome blue-and-white-tiled arabesques, the easiest to recognize.

Freshly picked mint leaves are a staple, used daily to prepare tea. The leaves are washed, carefully stripped off the stalks, and steeped with gunpowder green tea and sugar in boiling water.

Two women visit in Taroudant, ancient capital of the Sous region. Like many rural women, they observe

traditional head-to-toe garments in public.

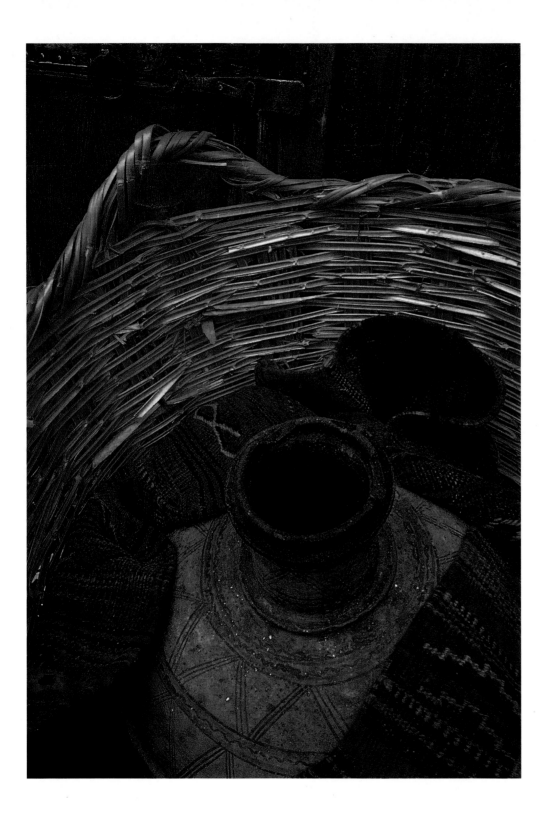

LEFT: A simple terra-cotta vase sits in a basket, wrapped in a colorful woven kilim. Pottery like this, employed for storing household needs such as food or water or for cooking, is made in rural areas by male potters. Folklore holds that the potter's workshop is sacred—should another take his place, the vessels would break overnight. Pottery can be brightly glazed or, as in this picture, plain with only basic designs scratched into the surface before firing.

OPPOSITE: Neatly folded inside out, knotted and woven Berber rugs are stacked ceiling-high in a merchant's shop. One by one, they will be unfolded to tempt an interested buyer, until the floor is covered with layer upon layer of carpets, which dazzle with an array of geometric designs.

ABOVE: Sweet red paprika and turmeric are essential ingredients in Moroccan cuisine,
lending both flavor and color to a multitude of meat and vegetable dishes.
The culinary variety of Moroccan food is extraordinary, and is often compared to
the great food traditions of France and China.

RIGHT: The sultan Mulay Ismail, builder of Meknès, is remembered at this shrine.
Ruling between 1672 and 1727, he was known for his fierce domination over his subjects and
for his grandiose building projects. His reputation for grandeur rivaled that of his European
contemporary Louis XIV; he tried to surpass the French king with a harem of five hundred
wives, and a workforce of thirty thousand slaves and twelve thousand horses.

Approaching Fez from the vast, almost
flat farmlands to the west of
the city, the impression is one of sheer
mystery. The medieval walls of Fez
appear like a mirage, and once through
the city gate, a bewildering density of
houses, narrow streets, and traffic
seem to swallow the visitor.

PHOTO CREDITS

©Dan Aubry: endpapers, 42–43, 55, 58–59

Aurora: ©Chris Anderson: 92–93; ©Beth Wald: 48

Corbis: ©Yann Arthus-Bertrand: 18, 23; ©Patrick Bennett: 69; ©James Davis: 84; ©Gerard Degeorge: 16; ©Wolfgang Kaehler: 24; ©Christine Osborne: 96; ©Arthur Thevenart: 85; ©Sandro Vannini: 80; ©Francesco Venturi: 28; ©Patrick Ward: 13; ©K.M. Westermann: 14, 68

©Lisl Dennis: 1, 2–3, 5, 7, 12, 17, 35, 38, 40, 47, 50, 51, 53, 56, 57, 60, 62, 63, 64–65, 66, 72, 73, 74, 76, 77, 78–79, 81, 83, 86, 87, 88, 89, 90

FPG International: ©Travelpix: 75

©Robert Fried: 25, 37, 45, 64, 78

©Robert Holmes: 34

Leo de Wys, Inc.: ©Donald Graham: 70–71; ©Sipa Image: 8–9; ©Siegfried Tauqueur: 11, 20, 46–47, 49; ©Steve Vidler: 44

©Craig Lovell: 39

Panos Pictures: 4; ©Jean-Leo Dugast: 30–31, 36–37; ©Jeremy Horner: 27, 54–55, 66–67, 90–91

Tony Stone: ©Glen Allison: 32; ©John Beatty: 41; ©Gerard Del Vecchio: 32–33, 82; ©Sylvain Grandadam: 52

Woodfin Camp & Associates: ©Robert Frerck: 60–61